YOUR KNOWLEDGE HAS VALUE

Bibliographic information published by the German National Library:

The German National Library lists this publication in the National Bibliography; detailed bibliographic data are available on the Internet at http://dnb.dnb.de .

Imprint:

Copyright © 2014 GRIN Verlag, Open Publishing GmbH
Print and binding: Books on Demand GmbH, Norderstedt Germany
ISBN: 978-3-668-05014-3

This book at GRIN:

http://www.grin.com/en/e-book/306807/descartes-and-the-cogito-our-foundation-of-philosophical-knowledge

Caden Sumner

Descartes and the "Cogito". Our Foundation of Philosophical Knowledge

GRIN Publishing

GRIN - Your knowledge has value

Since its foundation in 1998, GRIN has specialized in publishing academic texts by students, college teachers and other academics as e-book and printed book. The website www.grin.com is an ideal platform for presenting term papers, final papers, scientific essays, dissertations and specialist books.

Visit us on the internet:

http://www.grin.com/

http://www.facebook.com/grincom

http://www.twitter.com/grin_com

Descartes and the *Cogito*: Our Foundation of Philosophical Knowledge

Caden Sumner

St. Mary Lake Leelanau

March 13, 2015

Abstract

Synthesizing information from various sources, this paper reflects upon the life of René

Descartes, as well as the results of his work. Efficacy of Descartes' postulation is concluded in

relation to the impact made upon the world, citing present reflections of the statement "*Cogito,

Ergo Sum*". The history of Descartes' early life, his progression into philosophy, and modern

influences are utilized to portray his greatest work, and profound effects upon the world. The

importance of the *Cogito* is discussed in depth and in relation to modern society's interpretation

of Cartesian philosophy. The background of Cartesian philosophy, explanations of the process,

and meaning of ideas, serve to define the crux of the *Cogito* itself. Several postulates of famous

philosophers contradicting Descartes' ideas of solipsism are included, as well as modern

interpretations by famous authors, such as David Foster Wallace.

Keywords: knowledge, philosophy, René Descartes, Cogito Ergo Sum, Descartes

Descartes and the *Cogito*: Our Foundation of Knowledge

Prior to the revelations put forth by René Descartes, many philosophers operated under the presumptions that observance was knowledge in an objective sense. The profound statement *"Cogito, Ergo Sum"* that Descartes proposed truly defines the extent of all objective human knowledge. This proposition sheds light upon what the human consciousness may be, and the limitations that surround knowledge as a whole. The ideas of consciousness and reality were poured over in full detail by renowned philosophers long before Descartes. However, despite their efforts throughout history, no other philosopher was credited with producing the ideas that Descartes had. His propositions and postulates spark conversation among modern philosophers, writers, and laypeople, even to this day.

René Descartes: Early Life

Philosophical works tend to build upon the ideas of their predecessors. Oftentimes, instead of proposing entirely original ideas, philosophers will take ideas and reform them. One such example of philosophical reformation is Alexandrian Plotinus, as he had done in the case of Plato's early philosophies. Plotinus' alterations and adaptations of Plato's work later became known as Neoplatonism. In similar fashion, St. Augustine of Hippo reformed Plotinus' ideas in order to apply them into a working Christian philosophy. Philosophy is a field that is in a state of constant metamorphosis, continuous changes and additions renew ideas and allow philosophy as a whole to prosper. Although great changes in philosophy occurred before the time of Descartes, very few original works emerged. Alterations, additions, and corrections to previous philosophical ideas occupied the majority of history, but few groundbreaking innovations had arose. That is, until the work of Descartes was published to the world, bringing with it new ideas of fundamental knowledge (Strathern).

On March 31, 1596, René Descartes was born to a farmer in the traditional French province of Touraine. Descartes' mother had died when he was only one year old. Soon after, his father Joachim remarried and left Descartes to be raised by his grandmother, and eventually by his great-uncle. Caught in a familial turmoil, Descartes began to undertake formal education at a Jesuit college in La Flèche, France. After spending intermittent periods of time attending various universities and travelling Europe, he eventually found himself in the Netherlands at a college in Franeker (Watson). In 1628 Descartes began his philosophical career, at age 30, while simultaneously delving into research of both mathematics and the natural sciences.

Descartes' *Meditations on First Philosophy*, published in 1641, is made up of six separate *Meditations* in which Descartes begins by discarding all previously assumed knowledge or certainties. From this point forward, Descartes constructs new standards of fundamental knowledge and applies processes to verify information in an objective sense. In his first *Meditation* Descartes shares the following with readers of his work:

> It is some years now since I realized how many false opinions I had accepted as true from childhood onwards, and that, whatever I had since built on such shaky foundations, could only be highly doubtful. Hence I saw that at some stage in my life the whole structure would have to be utterly demolished, and that I should have to begin again from the bottom up if I wished to construct something lasting and unshakeable in the sciences. But this seemed to be a massive task, and so I postponed it until I had reached the age when one is as fit as one will ever be to master the various disciplines. Hence I have delayed so

long that now I should be at fault if I used up in deliberating the time that is left for

acting. The moment has come, and so today I have discharged my mind from all its cares,

and have carved out a space of untroubled leisure. I have withdrawn into seclusion and

shall at last be able to devote myself seriously and without encumbrance to the task of

destroying all my former opinions. (p. 17)

Descartes had used doubt as a tool, he forced it from his mind whilst deriving incontrovertible

knowledge, based upon the Cartesian doubt method of deductive reasoning. This allowed

Descartes the ability to begin formulating a basis of which only intrinsic, foundational

knowledge would stand.

Philosophy of *"Cogito, Ergo Sum"*

In order for Descartes to have a fresh outlook on the ideas of certainty and knowledge, he

had to throw away all preconceptions of knowledge that he had previously considered concrete

or inherently truthful. The first beliefs Descartes rejected were those relating to the senses.

Mainly, the idea that one believes in the existence of their own body, and everything that is

observed by sight and touch. Because these senses are subjective, and can be present in dreams,

they are discredited as fallacial knowledge. Descartes had often used the metaphor of a demon,

or malevolent being controlling his life. Similar to the analogy of dreaming, Descartes would not

be able to distinguish what in his life was created by the demon, and what was certain reality; his

observations, knowledge, and possibly even his own ideas were subject to fabrication by an

insidious force. Descartes was one of the first Philosophers to avail the word "idea" for his

philosophies, using the definition of "whatever the mind directly perceives". Because of this

definition, an idea may exist as a method of thought, however not necessarily as a truthful reality

(Roth).

According to *World Philosophers and Their Works*, Descartes was an avid proponent of deductive methods. He firmly upheld the belief that any form of knowledge, in order to be objective, must follow a set of principles. By applying this method, the idea of an "objective reality" was formulated. Descartes' method, used widely by philosophers of the time as well as modern philosophers, follows the following four step criteria:

1. Never accept any idea as true that is not so clearly and distinctly true as to be beyond all possibility of being doubted.

2. Divide each complex question into simple ones.

3. Order thoughts from the simplest to the most complex.

4. Review the series of inferences to make sure there are no breaks or false links in the chain.

These principles would also adhere to the first *Meditation* Descartes began to formulate and his beginning thoughts of knowledge. The first step in the process that he proposed is possibly what had lead Descartes to throw away all preconceived knowledge in order to start anew, from a purely logical and processed progression of thought. This objective stance would likely lend way to only the truth, and sift out any false or uncertain knowledge along the way. The crux of Descartes efforts resulted in an idea that provides the foundation for knowledge.

The origins of the famous *"Cogito, Ergo Sum"* finds itself amidst a harsh Bavarian winter. Writings from Descartes describe the frigid conditions from which his most famous piece of knowledge flourished. "Winter set in, and I found myself in a spot where there was no society of any interest. At the time I was unworried by any cares or passions, so I took to spending my day in a stove, where I could be alone with my thoughts". Although originally controversy surrounded whether or not Descartes resided in a literal oven (which was later to be assumed factual), there is no doubt that Descartes' ideas shifted humanities view on philosophy forever. Alone and secluded, he was left to nothing but his own mind, and under the circumstances he concluded the following: "there is just one thing that is undeniable: I am thinking. This alone proves to me my existence" (Strathern).

The phrase written above was later reduced into the Latin "*Cogito, Ergo Sum*", modernly known as "I think, Therefore I Am". The argument finds its basis in the idea of self-validation. By questioning whether oneself exists, he is validating his own existence. This is due to the fact that if oneself did not exist, there would be nothing to question. The *Cogito* uses this logic in order to establish a certainty in one thing: that "I" exists. Because Descartes focused a great majority of his energy into epistemological theories within his *Meditations*, it is of no surprise that the ideas of knowledge were explored in depth. Descartes has expressed that he has spent months pondering even the most basic of ideas in order to reach his conclusions. The idea that anything apart from one's own existence is unsure has been named "solipsism" from the Latin words meaning "alone" and "self" (Harper).

Proposed Opposition to the *Cogito*

Descartes's solipsistic ideas seemingly contradict the long-discussed idea of dualism. Dualism is a philosophy that emphasizes a substantial difference between the mind and the body. Some dualists even go as far as to say they are composed of entirely different materials. However, "*Cogito, Ergo Sum*" doesn't differentiate from mind and body, and states that anything outside of the mind cannot be seen as verifiable, or certain knowledge. This contradiction to the dichotomy of mind and body, conflicts with another theory of Descartes' known as "Cartesian dualism". This dualistic theory proposes that the mind is indivisible and eternal, even after the divisible or mortal body perishes. With this theory the assumption is made that the body is of existence, in a dynamic union with the soul, however the *Cogito* doesn't support that conclusion. Even before criticisms point out potential flaws, Descartes' own philosophy begins to show a non sequitur pattern.

A significant argument to Cartesian dualism, as well as dualism as a whole, comes from philosopher Thomas Hobbes. Hobbes argues that all human experiences, thoughts, and emotions, are biologically derived. In *The Leviathan* Hobbes concluded:

> The cause of sense is the external body, or object, which presseth the organ proper to each sense, either immediately, as in the taste and touch; or mediately, as in seeing, hearing, and smelling: which pressure, ... And this seeming, or fancy, is that which men call sense; and consisteth, as to the eye, in a light, or colour figured; to the ear, in a sound; to the nostril, in an odour; to the tongue and palate, in a savour; and to the rest of the body, in heat, cold, hardness, softness, and such other qualities as we discern by feeling. (p. 1)

Hobbes' ideas in *The Leviathan* go against both the *Cogito* as well as Dualism in the the sense that the body verifies the mind, and not vice versa as Descartes had theorized. Hobbes' approach to the idea of how consciousness works was strictly scientifically oriented, with little room for the more abstract thoughts Descartes had entertained.

Several philosophers have criticized the logic Descartes had used in the *Cogito* as well, based on Descartes practice of alluding to the "I" without first proving the existence of "I". The presumptions used that "I" inherently exists results in fallacial logic. As philosopher Bertrand Russell said in *An Outline of Philosophy* (1927):

> What, from [Descartes'] own point of view, he should profess to know is not 'I think,' but 'there is thinking'.... I think we ought to admit that Descartes was justified in feeling sure that there was a certain occurrence, concerning which doubt was impossible; but he was not justified in bringing in the word 'I' in describing this occurrence. (p. 130)

Because we lack any direct certainty that the "I" or *Cogito* form exists as it stands, the *Cogito* itself has been compromised during the postulation of the philosophy.

A more directly rebuffing criticism resounds from Scottish philosopher John Macmurray. In *The Self as Agent* Macmurray proclaims "We must reject this, both as standpoint and as method. If this be philosophy, then philosophy is a bubble floating in an atmosphere of unreality" (p. 78). Unlike Russell, Macmurray outright denounced the validity of Descartes' logic. Despite the varied reception of Descartes ideas, modern philosophy has been greatly influenced by the *Cogito* as well as its contributions to solipsism.

Modern Attributions

Modern philosophers and writers continue to discuss ideas originating from the *Cogito* to this day. Writers such as David Foster Wallace, famous for the encyclopedic novel *Infinite Jest*, have publicly stated ideas such as solipsism are a negative impact to society. Wallace warns that solipsism is harmful to upcoming generations, "... today's subforties have very different horrors, prominent among which are anomie and solipsism and a peculiarly American loneliness: the prospect of dying without even once having loved something more than yourself" (p. 54). Wallace expresses his concern that solipsism is an ideology abhorrent to the wellbeing of society, and a philosophical construct that lends to negative worldviews. Stances such as these on solipsism are rare, and commonly not as steadfast.

Many other philosophers however, view the ideas of solipsism and the *Cogito* as essential to modern thinking. These individuals view the postulates as necessary to bring the "self" into philosophy. The "self" in philosophy is invaluable, as it gives philosophical backing to the idea of "the world is my world". This subjective reality encompasses a plethora of new philosophical ideas, questions, and issues. Greatly expanding the scope of modern philosophy and extending outward to various other fields. Such fields include psychology; which studies personality and emotions, as well as a newly formed field of noetics which studies consciousness (Mounce).

Descartes epistemological concepts have positively altered modern thinking. Descartes challenged the world to follow a rigorous process to discern the truth, established ideas of solipsism that lead to further research into fields of subjective reality, and inevitably shifted the philosophical norm. From as far back as Plato, ideas that multiple senses of reality existed, were theorized. Plato's Theory of Forms established similar Cartesian ideas, however not nearly as extensive or flushed out as the *Cogito* (Liu). For philosophy to flourish, original theories such as the *Cogito* must be published, and shared for public discussion. If Descartes had been too fearful to release his *Meditations*, philosophy, and the world, would likely be altered forever.

References

Boyle, D. A. (2009). *Descartes on innate ideas*. London ; New York : Continuum, c2009.

Gaukroger, S. (1995). *Descartes: an intellectual biography*. Oxford :

    Clarendon Press ; Oxford ; New York : Oxford University Press, 1995.

Harper, D. (n.d.). Online Etymology Dictionary. Retrieved from

    http://www.etymonline.com/index.php?term=solipsism

Liu, P. (2013). *On Plato's theory of forms*. Canadian Social Science, (4), 206.

Macmurray, J. (1991). *The Self as Agent*. Humanity books.

Moriarty, M. (2008). *Meditations on First Philosophy : With Selections from the*

    Objections and Replies (René Descartes, Trans.) Oxford, GBR: Oxford University Press,

    UK.

Mounce, H. O. (1997). Philosophy, Solipsism and Thought. The Philosophical Quarterly, (186).

1.

Roth, J. (2000). *World philosophers and their works*. Pasadena, Calif.: Salem Press.

Russell, B. (1927). An outline of philosophy,. London: G. Allen & Unwin.

Strathern, P. (1996). *Descartes in 90 minutes*. Chicago : I.R. Dee, c1996.

Sorell, T. (2000). *Descartes : A Very Short Introduction*. Oxford, GBR: Oxford University

    Press, UK.

Stone, J. (1993). Cogito Ergo Sum. *The Journal of Philosophy*, (9). 462.

Wallace, D. F. (2006). "Certainly the End of Something or Other, One Would Sort of Have to

    Think (Re John Updike's Toward the End of Time)." Consider the Lobster and Other

Essays. New York: Little, Brown.

Watson, R. (2015). Encyclopædia Britannica. René Descartes.